Dominique J. Fryar

# Sermons

## *for the*

# Battlefield

**9 ways to reach God's Purpose and Plan
for Your Life**

iUniverse, Inc.
Bloomington

**Sermons For The Battlefield**
**9 ways to reach God's Purpose and Plan for Your Life**

iUniverse books may be ordered through booksellers or by contacting:

iUniverse
1663 Liberty Drive
Bloomington, IN 47403
www.iuniverse.com
1-800-Authors (1-800-288-4677)

ISBN: 978-1-4620-1824-6 (sc)
ISBN: 978-1-4620-1825-3 (e)

Printed in the United States of America

iUniverse rev. date: 03/05/2012

# The Preface

## Show Destiny You Are Worth It

We look at worthiness and see traits of honor, trust, and charity (which is also love). He that is honest and deserving of worthiness gets the reward of destiny. Just like the world is looking for worthy candidates to hold high positions in esteemed businesses and corporations, God is looking for a set apart people devoted to serve Him; God wants to raise a generation worthy to take the destiny of His ministry into the world to be a blessing. A generation that does not start with the adults, but starts with the children making it imperative that this generation make a stand to stop unworthiness and start showing honor and charity unto God. James was a practical man, he did not "sugarcoat" anything he told it like it was and kept within the Scriptures. So I will keep it simple, practical, but also scriptural. I am tired of books being published, and they do not have any power to help change a life (truly influence someone to change the way they think to achieve true spiritual prosperity and destiny power). The people read these books and really take in what is written on the pages reading about how many blessings they will get according to how much money is given, that is not Scripture. Power is not in the stock market, it is not in how many houses we can buy, sale or hold, power is not found in how many Grammies you have or top songs on the chart, but true power is in the faith of the seed that was sown through the promises of God and the shedding of blood by the Son of God-Jesus.

For there is only one church, but many members, and if we can help someone to reach their purpose and accomplish their mission in God, then we are overcomers together. Say to yourself, "SELF, I SHALL OVERCOME, what I am going through is only releasing my destiny into God's purpose for my life. God said, "Put them in fear, oh Lord; that the nations may know themselves to be but men" (Psalms 9: 20). We need to go back to fearing the Lord in order to respect His process. Our priorities are turned backwards; we will fear our friends and what they can do to us, but we will not fear God. There is one greater than your parent's greater than law enforcement and any military force on this earth and His name is Jesus the Christ. There is one that David spoke of in Psalms 8 when he said, "When I consider thy heavens. The works of thy fingers, the moon and the stars which thou hast ordained: what is man that thou art mindful of him?" We must continue to be steadfast in the standards of holiness and unwavering in our righteous thinking. We are charged to be different, and to show others that do not know the way, how to reach their greatest potential and live a spiritually prosperous life. God is calling every man to him. He is calling those that are strung out on drugs to put the addiction down and worship him. He is calling the young men to come off the street corner pull up their pants, throw down the guns and forsake the life of fast money, exquisite cars, and the likes of fleshly desires. The Lord has room in the kingdom for those willing to lose their life to gain eternal life and achieve spiritual prosperity.

Everyone is worried about life here on earth, but I challenge you not to worry about this world nor anything in it. I challenge you to focus on the life that is to come. Authors, ministers, theologians and pastors would worry about telling you how to get "earthly riches "but forget to tell you how to be Rich in favor, love and grace (all yielding the divine pursuit of happiness, prosperity and eternal salvation for your life). My dear brothers and sisters do not conform to this world and do not let this world influence you into selling your body, dealing or using drugs or given into fleshly desires that will only cloud your mind from receiving the true and loving Will of God. You are more important than the drugs, sex, fast money and squandered promises the world stage presents. You have more value than to allow yourself to be misused by society only to be discarded after the "spotlight" is done with you. Trust God and let him show you the true way.

Forgiveness goes a long way. It starts in your heart and releases into your mind. We must make up in our mind that we are going to live for God and make up in or heart that we will be faithful to the destiny of our life. Show God you are faithful, accountable and teachable; this will make for a much larger spiritual increase. Do not make up excuses to justify your wrongdoing, instead admit those mistakes and learn from them. Do not expect a pity party to get you back on the right track. We all know how to pray, we all know what we need and all we have to do is humble ourselves and ask God to show us His way and show us how not to think we are less on His list because we are misusing our lives. So what you pray more than others. True worthiness starts with accountability, wanting to be told your faults, wanting to have to answer to God. Do you think that you are the only one fasting three times a week to fight off the temptations of this world? No, you are not, matter of fact you must continue this practice of praying to obtain help from the Father to show you how to reach your full capacity; spiritual prosperity is not earned overnight. We must set the standards for future generations. We must set the bar for our children and their children. "A sewer went out to sow his seed: and as he sowed, some fell by the wayside; it was trodden down, and the flies of the air devoured it. In addition, some fell upon a rock; and as soon as it was sprung up, it withered away because it lacked moisture. And some fell among thorns and the thorns sprang up with it, and choked it. Another fell on good ground, and sprang up and bear fruit one hundred fold"- Luke 8. Do not be like the one who sowed on the rock, do not be like the one who sowed and it falls by the wayside. And definitely do not be like the one who sowed and found his seeds falling among the thorns. We need to be sowing on good ground, so that our seeds can be rooted and grounded for our increase.

Make up in your mind you are going to be the one Jesus talks about sowing on good ground-ground fit for territory enlargement and destiny strengthening . We all have a purpose in this life and that purpose is directly linked to God's preordained destiny plan for us. There is a "life plan" that has already been registered and cataloged for you, but we get too busy trying to rewrite the manuscript for our self. Every word written by God is linked with a blessing and sealed with a promise. The answers we are looking for can be found in the Dogma and God-breathed literature of our Bibles. God is looking for a remnant of people that will stand on his doctrine and the truths of His Word. A generation that is tired of planting on unworthy ground and ready to plant to the glory of God the Father and allow the increase of the kingdom of God to decrease the desires of their flesh. While there is no substitution for the reading of the Word of God, we can share principles and Godly insight on the scriptures to help perfect the Body of Christ. For the Bible does say "We are overcome by our testimonies". So, Composed in these next series of chapters are truths or principles, revealed to me from Biblical scriptures, to help see the purpose and plan God has on our life. So grab your pen and a Bible and let us look at what God is trying to tell us. Do not worry who you are or what you have done in life, God wants to transform every destiny into Godly purpose in whosoever is willing to let Him do it. Say this with me "GOD WANTS TO RELEASE MY DESTINY INTO HIS PURPOSE!" Say it again, "GOD WANTS TO RELEASE MY DESTINY INTO HIS PURPOSE! Are you ready to be transformed? Are you ready for a change? Are you ready to let go and let God? Then let go, and authorize the Holy Spirit to release in you knowledge, purpose, understanding, love, peace and happiness as you read, study and listen to what He has to say to you today.

## Spiritual Prosperity Diagram

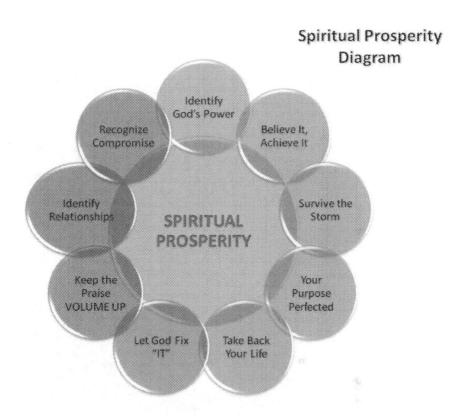

*Spiritual Prosperity Diagram*

Dedicated to the Fryar family and the entire House of God COGIC family. Mom without you there would not have been a Dominique. To Bishop Mark Walden and Mother Dorothy Walden thank you for teaching and preaching the Word and being there for me and my family. To my mentor Elder Mark Walden, thank you for the in-depth studying that has helped me find the road of perfecting what God has given me. To my BIG Brother Elder Jimmie Sturgis thank you for your practical, thought provoking and applicable knowledge in everything I do, it might be tight, but it is right and I thank you. To Jimmie Barnett NCOIC of pharmacy operations at the Fort Gordon Refill Pharmacy, thank you for the motivation and encouragement you gave me while I was writing this book. Most of all I want to thank my wife "Niecey" for her longsuffering and unconditional love for me and her faithfulness in God that this vision would come to pass- Thanks babe you give me hope every day. I thank you all from the bottom of my heart!

# TABLE OF CONTENTS

# Chapter 1

*Identifying God's Power*

### *"Press to Activate"*

Scripture: Matthew 21:23-27

**"A**nd when he was come into the temple, the chief priests and the elders of the people came unto him as he was teaching, and said, By what authority doest thou these things? and who gave thee this authority? And Jesus answered and said unto them, I also will ask you one thing, which if ye tell me, I in like wise will tell you by what authority I do these things. The baptism of John, whence was it? from heaven, or of men? And they reasoned with themselves, saying, If we shall say, From heaven; he will say unto us, Why did ye not then believe him? But if we shall say, Of men; we fear the people; for all hold John as a prophet. And they answered Jesus, and said, We cannot tell. And he said unto them, Neither tell I you by what authority I do these things.*

If you want to, you can add on whatever you desire to this chapter's title. You can use God's power to live. You can use God's power to talk right. You can even use God's power to think right. Power! It was by the supreme authority of God that Jesus had the right to do, say and preach all that he did. This is what is needed, and this is what is lacking in society today, the

Power of God. We find ourselves thinking weak and planning meager lives for ourselves. When we start a new job we are full of God's grace and power only to get weak as the years toil on. We are trained to become relaxed and give in to the "this is how it will always be" mentality. Someone might have started a relationship meant right in the beginning, but came up short in so many areas at the end. I would say they lost power somewhere during the relationship. Some may have started out focusing on the Lord, praying like they should, reading and studying like they should, but the enemy came, and they began to second-guess themselves. I would say they need more power. Why do they need more power you ask? They need power to fight this never ending war between flesh and Spirit. Power is needed to fight off all forces of demonic influence both in us and around us. Our communication needs to have power. Our actions need to have power. Our thinking needs to be full of power. We are living strenuous lives and living beneath our privileges, if we do not have the power of God abiding in our lives.

Too many times in life do we witness people that do not have power. We see this in the workforce, in relationships, in marriages, in businesses and we can even see it in the lives of some of God's people. So why as Christian Soldier are we afraid to fight? We need to get back to the power that created everlasting blessings instead of trying to recreate a new power to create temporary blessings-keep reading! We have something to do ourselves; everything has a price-nothing is free? According to the New Bible Dictionary, Third Edition power represents chiefly the Greek meaning *dynamis* and *exousia*. *Exousia* means derived or conferred 'authority', the warrant or right to do something (Mt. 21:23-27); from this it comes to denote concretely the bearer of authority on earth (Rom. 13:1-3), or in the spirit world (Col. 1:16). *Dynamis* is ability (2 Cor. 8:3) or strength (Ephesians 3:16), or it may mean a powerful act (Acts 2:22) or a powerful spirit (Rom. 8:38). Christ had all authority given him by his Father (Mt. 28:18) and he used it to forgive sins (Mt. 9:6) and to cast out evil spirits (Mt. 10:1). He gave authority to his disciples to become sons of God (Jn. 1:12) and to share in his work (Mk. 3:15)." Webster goes on to tell us power is an influence; it is a type of strength we have to motivate or persuade. He also tells us that it is an influential person, but never tells us who this person is. We know that people like Nelson Mandela, Dr. Martin Luther King, President Bill Clinton and TD Jakes all have a form of influence. Power does not lie in these prominent figures, even though they have a form of influence and some of them even have a form of power, the definition tells us that there is one influential person that has power. This person takes care of your finances. This influential person takes care of pain, sickness, heartaches, even unbelief. So where does this power come from? From whence did this power exist? Have you only a second-hand knowledge of this influential person that has incredible influential power on every aspect of our destiny and faith? If your answer is yes I propose a question, have you ever tried Jesus? Jesus is He who the scriptures say has all power in heaven and in earth. It is Jesus that came to the world with all authority in His hand- Jesus, Jesus, Jesus. If you answered no to this question I ask you a question. What or who is keeping you from allowing this power to work in your life? The Bible tells us, neither is their power in any other, for at the name of Jesus every knee shall bow and every tongue confess that He is Lord-stop waiting on God to control your life and start letting God control your life.

If you have lowered your standards and have shown yourself to be powerless, ask God for help. God wants to increase your life to increase His witness in you. God wants to do more for you than you could ever promise Him you could do. So just ask God to help you and believe in the hope of His help. Ask so that your power can be restored from that which is wide of the mark, to that which is dead centered on the mark of Christ Jesus. If you have been walking in the power of Godly purpose on your way to your destiny and have kept steadfast in our Lord and Savior Jesus Christ you are traveling the road to the power of spiritual prosperity and destiny in the Lord. It is the power of the Holy Spirit, which comes to destroy every "dead" thing in your life and restores the vision in your heart. It is written that after you receive the Holy Ghost that you shall also receive power. I beseech ye therefore, brethren by the mercies of God, that if you do not have this power I speak of, quickly seek God for the liberation that rest in repentance and ask God to fill the void in your life with the presence of His glory and Holy Spirit. The destiny we search for daily awaits us, hanging in the balance of our passions and talents. Once we figure out (through God) the power of our passion and pair that passion with faith and trust in the power of God's total plan- destiny then awakens in us. God holds us responsible with every gift He blesses us with. He holds us accountable to share these gifts to enhance the Kingdom. I have been charged to write to His people to open up understanding and share the knowledge of my experience. When I allowed the power of destiny to collide with God's purpose in my life the passion to help others and share my life lessons came to surface in my heart. From my studies, I learned there are three types of people. The first types do not have power. The second type are those that have power and are not using it and the third type of person is the person that has power, using it, loving it and know they have it. Which type are you?

Those persons that fall in category number one need to stay on their knees praying and asking God to give them more power. God tells us in Luke 24:49 in the latter portion of the Scripture "*....tarry ye in the city of Jerusalem, until you receive power from on high*". This verse gives us the assurance that Christ will show up when we trust in him, and we wait on the source of our strength. When we find ourself powerless, we tend to feel useless, easily agitated and sometimes withdrawn. When active power is not in our life, we will not be able to actively function. Those that are in category number two are the most dangerous. Just like Moses, we sometimes have the source of our destiny in our hand but we refuse to listen to God's instructions on how to use it. We complain and make excuses trying to find any and every way out, but just like God told Moses to use what was in his possession to get him to his position, I encourage you to listen to the same words God gave Moses and use what God has placed in your hands. We must put into action the words that God speaks to us in order to see his power manifests in our lives. Power is something everyone wants, but when we do receive some type of authority, we use it for the wrong reasons. A person that has purpose and does not share it is dangerous. They are telling you, God and me that they do not have faith in the knowledge or authority given to them by God. If God did not get hold on Moses' thinking Israel would of never made it (if the decision was left up to Moses)-Moses did not believe what he possessed in his hands was the solution to the problem-But do you know God always has a way that will "blow" us away? The Bible tells us there is a way that seemeth right to me, but the end thereof, is death. Yes, we may reap benefits of riches and gain recognition on this earth, but the pride of a powerless man will lead him to destruction. And without the Holy Ghost power our destiny will never collide with the true purpose of our existence. No matter how many mottos, slogans, or aphorisms we use we must still rely on God. The only slogan and plan for our lives should be the plan left for us by Jesus. If it is not Jesus than who can deliver us from sin? If it is not Jesus who can prosper us as our soul prospers? If we do not trust on Jesus, than who are we trusting in? Even in a career, to find joy we must rely on the power of Christ. Coworkers will try your patience to see if your patience is really going to longsuffer with them; people will "test" you. Work can and will "work" on your last nerve to see if you have nerve enough to pray instead of prey. You may already be having a terrible day, got a lot on your mind, not feeling well or just aggravated. The enemy does not care. So why should we care about the enemy? The easy answer is we should not care about anything our adversary has for us. The only way to win a spiritual war is to use spiritual weapons. Use your spiritual gifts and weapons to combat Satan's main weaponry; lust of the flesh, lust of the eyes and the pride of life. Satan has been using these three weapons since the Garden of Eden. He has so much faith in his weapons he even tried to use them on God and then again on Jesus. The enemy wants us to feel sorry for ourself and wants us to start thinking for ourself, instead of allowing the wisdom of God to guide us. You may say to yourself, well I have been fornicating; drinking, smoking and or living a powerless way of living all my life so why stop now? The answer to this thinking is because your adversary wants you to stay defeated and continue in the cycle of sin and repent, sin and repent, sin and repent. We should stop feeling sorry for ourself, dust yourself off and have joy in knowing that your opponent the Devil cannot keep you down. He may knock you down, but he has not knocked you out. Get back up and use the authority God has given you to assign a deadly blow to the Enemies camp. The word of God tells us that we are born in sin and God's son Jesus Christ of Nazareth came to save us from this sin. Do not think that your power will stop you from sinning-notice I said your power-because it will not. You must trust in the power of the living God to get you out of every situation. There is no time for feeling sorry for yourself. Just like the Prodigal Son went back on his father and his father forgave him, so much the more we must learn from the Prodigal Son (Luke chapter 15) and remember that the power of the all loving God will forgive us and accept us back from any situation, if we fully surrender to His Will. Use the power God has given you from the knowledge of your destiny. Get up and help somebody else. There is not a better person to learn from than somebody that has been through it, taken the bruises, worn the T-shirt and survived the storm. It is not time to feel sorry, but it is time that the children of God rejoice. Rejoice in the fact that God came to create purpose and fulfill destiny in your life. The heavens hold the power of the Only Begotten Son and whosoever beliveth on Him shall (this is a promise-SHALL) not perish, but have everlasting life-It is time to rejoice. We have to admit that bad times, tests, trials and tribulations will come, but the Word of God shall always prevail. When we use the Word of God, we will get through all of life's difficulties safely. If you want victory, you have got to do it God's way. If you want peace of mind you, have the peace of God dwelling on the inside. We must refrain from relying on our own understanding, but we must acknowledge God in all of our ways; recognize and depend on the authority in Him.

So the secret is out, as long as we keep God in our life and the blood of Jesus Christ over our life we do not have to worry about depression or a recession. Everything that you do must be ordered by God's holy power. Whatever you want; if you need power to live right, power to think right, power to love the right away then we need the power of God in our life. Hide in the secret place of God's anointing. This secret place of God is given to those that access the power of His sovereignty and walk in total submission to His Will.

# CHAPTER QUESTIONS

1. By what Supreme Authority did Jesus operate?

2. Why is it important to have the kind of power talked about in this chapter?

3. In this chapter, you learned a Greek word for power. What was that Greek term and how was it used throughout the bible?

4. What powerful act was talked about in Acts 2:22?

5. After reading this chapter, how are you going to use the power of God in your life?

# CHAPTER 2

*Believe It, Achieve It*

## *"How to reach Divine Purpose"*

Scripture: Hebrews 11:1-3

"*Now faith is the substance of things hoped for, the evidence of things not seen. For by it the elders obtained a good report. Through faith we understand that the worlds were framed by the word of God, so that things which are seen were not made of things which do appear.*"

Sin is a violation of conscience or the Divine Law. When we sin we are not fulfilling the divine purpose God has for our life. When we violate we infringe on God's plan and worry about things that we should not worry ourself with. We step on the "toes" of God when we disbelieve. Sin is not only a violation, but it is the outcome of being without faith. The writer Paul says in Romans 14:23, "he that doubts is damned if he eateth, because he eateth not of faith: for whatsoever is not faith is sin." Faith believes in the power of God, and if your motives are not faith-based then you do not believe in God to see you through. If your motives are not faith-based, you are not agreeing with the word of God that says I can do all things through Christ, which strengthens me. Sometimes we forget to pray when we are

going through a trial. When old things come back to haunt us and snare
our conscience to get us off track, we must not forget to humble ourselves
in the presence of his divinity. The Bible tells us that men ought to always
pray and in praying we are not to refrain from this discipline of spiritual
communication. So you ask how do I reach my destiny. You may ask, what
is my purpose here in Life. I would have to tell you to pray harder, for
God's divine purpose. Think about this, if prayer is direct connection to
God and God urges us to always pray, then God must want us to always be
connected to him. And if always connected to God, then as we pray more
we will be connected more and sin will have no choice but to pack up and
leave our life forever. What is prayer? Prayer is a humbling of your desires
in order to lean how God to operate fully in you and through you. Prayer
is a conversation between you and God. You cannot talk to anyone on
your phone if you've been disconnected. A pay phone will not work unless
you have the correct change or can use a phone card that has minutes on
it. Prayer is our operator that connects us directly to God. Necessarily,
no prayer cloth is needed. You do not necessarily need a prayer partner to
reach the throne of God. The Bible says that when Jesus was crucified for
our sins and rose again to give us life, that the Vail between him and man
was ripped. Therefore, if I sin, I automatically disconnect myself from the
power source of God. Sin temporarily disconnects my communication and
modifies the divine purpose of my life. Remember now that sin is a direct
violation of the conscience or the Divine Law. So in order to understand
the definition of sin we must understand what our conscience is. Man's
conscience is his moral sensitivity, doubts or uncertainty about what he
should or should not do. The word conscience is replaced with heart in
the Scriptures to signify the importance of man's thoughts over his life.
If then the heart is a vital organ in the body, without it blood could not
pump to our organs. Then without prayer the destiny in our life will not
release or "pump" into our purpose. If your heart is damaged there is
a slight chance of life remaining in that body. So, if your conscience is
your moral sensitivity and your heart is described as the center of man's
emotional storage and where difference of sensitivity is decided, than your
conscience is God's direct link to your heart and if your conscience is not

clear your heart cannot be pure and if your heart is impure how can you have faith in your connection if you have been disconnected from the conversation going on between your spirit and God? The book of Acts 24:16 says "in here and do I exercise myself but have always a conscience void of offense toward God and toward men." How can you have an offense or disagreement against your brother and say you are in contact with God? How can someone, a Christian, exemplifying Christ fix their conscience mind to agree with the misconception that they do not like someone? I encourage you in order to reach the divine purpose for your life we must pray harder. For if, we pray harder our conscience has no other choice but to let go of all the hatred and malice in our heart. Satan knows if he can attack your conscience and make it weak he can make our sin more contagious and make our witness of none affect. 1 Corinthians 8:6-7 says "But to us *there is but* one God, the Father, of whom *are* all things, and we in him; and one Lord Jesus Christ, by whom *are* all things, and we by him. "Howbeit *there is* not in every man that knowledge: for some with conscience of the idol unto this hour eat *it* as a thing offered unto an idol; and their conscience being weak is defiled." Do not allow your situation to outweigh your trust in the Lord. Jesus said, men ought always pray or to always be in connection with him. We see that sin is a violation or an infringe on the conscience and that prayer is a communication or the direct link to God through our conscience. So when we least expect it or do not realize it, we should be connected. Hebrews tells me that faith is the substance (the material of which anything is made or constituted) of things hoped (to desire something with competent expectation of its fulfillment) for and the evidence (that which make something clear; an outward sign or indication) of things not seen. We live by faith. We talk by faith. We walk by faith, and by hope we see the next day. However, when we are in direct violation of the Divine Law the evidence is unclear that we will live to see our destiny fulfilled, especially when our conscience mind is disconnected from God, not allowing God to control your central position in life. You know, without God we should never have made it this far, but the divine purpose God has for you told the enemy "have you tried my servant (enter your name here)? I know there is still someone on my earth that will stand up for righteousness and allow my purpose to be fulfilled. Confess today that the purpose in you shall live and not die and that your destiny shall be released. When we pray we do not know the desired or the undesired outcome, but pray to the point where your conscience and subconscious is in total communication with God. Then we will walk by faith and not by sight, this is when the destiny of a healing ministry in your life will take place. The lame will walk, blinded eyes will be opened. Prayer will shut the door to sinful communication and open the floodgates of divine intervention- Pray harder. This is when God can fully use you to fulfill his purpose through you-SHOUT DESTINY. When you have walked into your transformation and divinely purposed calling on your life. For I hear Paul saying, and be not conformed to this world but be transformed by the renewing of your mind that he may prove what is that good and acceptable and perfect will of God. Jesus and the enemy cannot dwell in the same place if they could Satan would still have a place in heaven. Your body is the temple of Christ and therefore if your body is the temple of the Spirit of God, any demonic force or principality you are battling with must come down. They can no longer control your conscience or play with your heart. If you would just pray, a little harder God's divine purpose for your life will come to pass-SHOUT DESTINY. We sit back and think about how to get rich, how to marry the one we love or how to make a life a little easier. Well, I come to tell you today that as long as you keep your eyes on the world and what it can offer you the darkness of confusion will always be present. The darkness of the world will sear your conscience therefore severing your heart's connection with God not allowing you to hear, think or perceive the way God wants you to go in order to release destiny into purpose. If you want to really know how to reach purpose and spiritual prosperity, it is easy-keep your eyes, heart and communication on God.

# CHAPTER QUESTIONS

1.  In this Chapter, sin is described as a violation of what?

2.  When we sin is it possible to still fulfill our divine purpose, why or why not?

3.  According to the scriptures and this chapter, what is sin?

4.  What is prayer?

5.  How can we keep our lines of communication open with God?

# CHAPTER 3

## Survive the Storms

*"Remember there is Sunshine after every storm"*
Scripture: Isaiah 12:2-6; Matthew 8:23-27.

**"B**ehold, God is my salvation; I will trust, and not be afraid: for the LORD JEHOVAH is my strength and my song; he also is become my salvation. Therefore with joy shall ye draw water out of the wells of salvation. And in that day shall ye say, Praise the LORD, call upon his name, declare his doings among the people, make mention that his name is exalted. Sing unto the LORD; for he hath done excellent things: this is known in all the earth. Cry out and shout, thou inhabitant of Zion: for great is the Holy One of Israel in the midst of thee."*

*And when he was entered into a ship, his disciples followed him. And, behold, there arose a great tempest in the sea, insomuch that the ship was covered with the waves: but he was asleep. And his disciples came to him, and awoke him, saying, Lord, save us: we perish. And he saith unto them, Why are ye fearful, O ye of little faith? Then he arose, and rebuked the winds and the sea; and there was a great calm. But the men marvelled, saying, What manner of man is this, that even the winds and the sea obey him!*

The cry for help goes out, but there isn't anyone around to hear it. You cry louder scream harder, but your voice is still unheard. Some may ask the question why does everything seem so right in the beginning and end so wrong? Seems like you are having test after test, storm after storm, and so much confusion that life begins to overflow. You do not want to feel this way, but you cannot help it. You tried to throw all your cares over board to keep from sinking. You tried to steer away from the storm to only find yourself moving in the direction of the storm's eye. Then sometimes you try to take on your own storms, but lack any knowledge or experience in how to weather a storm. When you think family is there to help we find they have jumped overboard with all of our cargo. Our friends that we once were able to find are now missing; swimming, right behind our family. At any other time, your family would be encouraging you telling you to go on, push ahead, don't give up. After your most vulnerable time, your family is found telling you to give up, but there is something about being able to survive the storm, especially when your help is the Lord Jesus Christ. You can count on Jesus seeing you through every test, trial, and tribulation. He is able. He who has made the heavens and the earth. He who stopped the storm from overtaking his disciples in St. Matthew 8:23-27 is the same God available to help you. We all know after a storm the sun does shine, it is no different for your storm-SHOUT, IT WILL SHINE. Isaiah 12 we witness the song of praise by the reading. God uses the prophet Isaiah, because of his literary ingenious. Isaiah's Hebrew name Yesh'-Yahu means God is salvation. Isaiah lets us know just by the meaning of his name that God is able. God will protect us, he will give us a way out of our situation. Even when we are constantly misunderstood, God understands us. When it seems like no matter how we express ourself or choose our words, God "gets" us. You always are misunderstood, and somebody is always unhappy but let us press to please the Master and stop worrying about the nay-Sayers on the sideline.

Do not for one moment think that walking with Christ will keep storms away or keep you away from seeking for happiness, because it is just the opposite. Being with Christ is better than anything you have experienced, but storms and trials are part of our perfection (maturation). Isaiah (Isaiah 12:2-6) behold, God is my salvation; I will trust, and not be afraid: for the Lord Jehovah is my strength and my song. Therefore with joy shall, ye draw water out of the wells of salvation. And in that day shall ye say, Praise the Lord, call upon his name, declare his doings among the people, make mention that his name is exalted. Sing unto the Lord; for he hath done excellent things: this is known in all the year. Cry out and shout thou inhabitant of Zion: for great is the Holy One of Israel in the midst of thee. David describes the Lord's goodness as sweet music played upon an instrument of ten strings. Psalms 92:3-6,"upon an instrument of 10 strings, and upon psaltery; upon the harp was the solemn sound. For thou, Lord has made me glad to thy word: I would try him in the works of thy hands. O Lord, how great are thy works! Plus thy thoughts are very deep. A brutish man know with not; neither does the misunderstood understand this." David lets us know that in God there is much safety, and much joy, peace and happiness. The fact is, anytime you feel safe. You should feel happy, and a sense of joy. For those of us that feel like we are weathering the storm all alone just know God is there. Feels like no one is praying with you or for you. Maybe it seems like so many things are coming up against you, just remember, Jesus is our rock. Remember even when deceitful friends and family come against you, cry out to Jesus, praise louder and louder every time your storm comes. When you scream the ears of men may be muffled but God is always listening. Pray like David did "Give ear to my prayer, O God; and hide not thy self from my supplication. Attend unto me, and hear me: I mourn in my complaint, and make a noise. Because of the voice of the enemy come because of the oppression of the wicked: for they cast iniquity upon, and in wrath they hate me." Your enemies do not care about you, they will try to do everything to make your life miserable. Try showing unconditional love even to your enemies; this will give you a sure blessing from God. When your enemies get to be too much for you trust in God to take care of them. When storms arise given them to Jesus. We have an arsenal of defense, and his name is Jesus. He who sits on the Right Hand of the Father making intercession for you and me. "As for me, I will call upon God; and the Lord shall save me" (Psalms 16).

Chosen of God, the generation of inheritors believe in your father, my dear brother rejoice because you know of a man that is able to prove you through your test, knowing it is not in how many women you have, happiness does not abide in the ship of fornication. It does not abide in the sand of lust, but it does abide in the ship you find Jesus sailing on. Because when a storm comes in and life rains heavily, if you're not on the Lord's ship, you shall sink. But upon a foundation, built on the chief cornerstone upon the stone the builders rejected we look back and see the life our forefathers (Abraham, Isaac and Jacob) had when they built on sandy ground, then look what happened when they built upon the rock, which is Jesus Christ. Jesus is who we should want to build on. We will come to understand what true joy is when God gives us sunshine after the storm. When it looks like the storm is going to get the best of us we will be able to make it through every storm. We will be able to come out with a story of victory and not a story of defeat. My sister do not rely on that man to give you happiness, do not rely on your career and do not rely on your money. For all material things will vanish, but if you have found Jesus, you have a guarantee of longevity. I come to encourage you to put your trust in God and not to man. Look to the Father and he will lead you to true and everlasting love. Peace abiding in us, if we trust in God. Jesus will do his part, Jesus will come through for you even if you don't ask Him to He will come to your rescue. Your ship may rock-just a little bit and it may even crack on one side and spring leaks you can't find, but knowing Jesus is there to keep the ship from rocking out of control, keep the cracks from ruining your ship and to find every leak. This is enough to say, Yes Lord, Yes I will.

God will come to your rescue every time, if we allow him to. Let them persecute, let them talk about you, let them treat you wrong all they want; man will get mad and will never forgive or forget. God forgives and God forgets and will give you sunshine after every storm, test and or trial even the ones we fail. I have survived my storm, the storm did not survive me. They have talked about me, they slandered my name, and they have misused me. Living in houses with what I thought to be family only to find out they were planting seeds of destruction, designed to destroy the very destiny birthed in me. Nothing would go right for me until I call Storm Tracker JESUS. Trying to love my father returned to me void at times. Trying to help my grandmother, I learned man's love is in money and not rooted in faith, but I am so glad to know that God's love rests in and last throughout eternity. I have survived the storm and want you to know you can survive your storm too. Do not let this storm (or any storm hereafter) abide in you or around you without abiding first with Jesus-As long as you abide in God and allow God to prepare you for your storm, you will always have a JOY after the storm.

# Chapter Questions

1.  What two scriptures are used in this Chapter?

2.  Meditate on these two scriptures and in your own words, how can these scriptures come to life in your present situation?

# Chapter 4

## Know who is Your Battle Axe?

*"Your Purpose is Perfected by His fight (not yours)"*
Scripture: 2Corinthians 10:1-5

*N*ow I Paul myself beseech you by the meekness and gentleness of Christ, who in presence am base among you, but being absent am bold toward you: But I beseech you, that I may not be bold when I am present with that confidence, wherewith I think to be bold against some, which think of us as if we walked according to the flesh. For though we walk in the flesh, we do not war after the flesh: (For the weapons of our warfare are not carnal, but mighty through God to the pulling down of strong holds;) Casting down imagination, and every high thing that exalteth itself against the knowledge of God, and bringing into captivity every thought to the obedience of Christ;

In this passage of scripture we see that Paul is explaining the significance of understanding, what kind of battle we are fighting. Verse one says "Now I Paul myself beseech you by the meekness and gentleness of Christ, who in the presence am base among you, but being absent am bold toward you. This gives us the author's writ or stamp of approval in the Scripture. I would like to look at the genitive form that was placed on verse 4. Where

Paul goes on to say, (for the weapons of our warfare are not carnal, but mighty through God to the pulling down of strongholds). The genitive is a word that restricts or justifies the purpose of the noun by giving it a specific characterization. The genitive usually marks the noun as the possessor or the proprietor of something. So knowing the definition of genitive and being able to break down this passage of scripture. We can see the word warfare is in the genitive qualifying weapons. Therefore, we know that we do have some type of weapons to do war with.

In my studies of the topic many battles were fought. The warriors gave God praise and all the credit for every victory. They did not complain or try to find fault if they lost. Most wars or battles fought in the Bible had some spiritual meaning like in 2 Corinthians 10:4. The writer Paul tells us for the weapons of our warfare are not carnal, but mighty through God to the pulling down of strongholds. Once the battle is fully given to God we must not worry about it anymore. The only serenity we have is in Christ. No matter how hard the battle may seem. David was not a strong man, but was not weak either. There was one type of soldier that was used in the Bible days until Solomon built a professional army through taxation and trading. This type of soldier was called a foot soldier. These foot soldiers volunteered to fight and in most cases were recorded as able-bodied men. They were the infantrymen of the Calvary and did all the work for the military. The able-bodied men did not have time to prepare their minds for war. They did not have time to prepare their heart or their emotions for the battle. Being a man in good physical condition was the most important qualification for the foot soldier. God gives us strength and the right mind to endure our warfare. How good is God? Are you able-bodied?

See we think that the one who fights and wins the battle dictates who is the strongest or who is the weakest. In this spiritual war it does not matter who is the weakest or strongest because the one that has Jesus Christ of Nazareth on their team understands that the spiritual battle is not fought between flesh and blood but is given to Jesus to fight for us. When you give your battle to Jesus, purpose flows. When you are a spiritual foot soldier treading over every serpent of your warfare, destiny is released. You have no other choice but to come out victorious. Knives, guns and fist are not the way to win this war. Do you understand that no matter how strong you think you are if God gives the situation the green light, it can and will destroy you. Do you know that it does not matter how weak and frail your opponent thinks you are, if you are prepared to fight and God hedges you there is no punch you cannot take and there is no battle that you cannot and will not win. War is a conscious thing; war is fought through our mind. If you are not mentally prepared to enter the battleground-no matter how much physical training you think you have, you will crack under pressure. You have to come out of yourself and allow the father to substitute and fortify you in your battle. You cannot let anyone know what you are doing in the battle-Just let JESUS fight! The military has this code called the phonic alphabet, where every letter is represented by a word. When used properly the enemy cannot understand what is being communicated between the soldiers and command. The only one that can understand this phonic alphabet is those that are on your side. God has a phonic system of his own, he has an attack plan that will confuse the enemy, and the only one that can understand it is those that are on His side. Instead of complaining about your current place you find yourself in and instead of walking in defeat I encourage you to walk in COMPLETE VICTORY- starting now. Walk in this victory, knowing that the battle is not yours, but it is the Lord's.

It may seems like you never get a break or can have a peace of mind. If it seems like every day you lose another portion of your joy or if it seems like you do not understand what is going on in your life. I would encourage you not to complain, because complaining is fighting with our flesh but praying is fighting in the spirit. Check this, If we allow our warfare, which is not carnal, to make us lose our mind then we have allowed the enemy to trick us out of our blessing. We must pray the prayer that God will replace our way of thinking with his divine way of thinking. We are bothered with trying to understand what God is trying to do in our life. We are trying to figure out how can we drive our destiny and purpose or what we are to do in our battles. God said that we have to go back to minding our own agenda. When you gave your life over to Christ and accepted him as your personal savior all of your problems were also given to Jesus. We must understand that life is no longer in our hands, but it now is the sole responsibility of God. In order for our purposes to be perfected by warfare we must not interfere with what God is trying to do for us and through us. The Bible tells us that many are the afflictions of the righteous but God delivers them [the righteous] out of them all, so no one ever told us that we would not have some troubles, but the Bible does tell us that we will not be overthrown by those troubles. When we interfere with the work of God, we end up making a mess that we are just going to ask God to clean up for us later. So spare the frustration; let go and let God. In this life there is only one thing you can do when all hope is lost-Hope in Jesus.

This life is all about choices. If you make the right choice you'll have peace of mind. Make the wrong choice you will feel as if you are a failure. Grief will set in, doubt will rise, anger will rest there and if you are not careful, you will try to fight this battle with anger. One thing I found out about God is in the time of perfecting God will sit back and allow us to pollute our situation. He is just waiting to see how long it takes for us to call on Him to clean up the pollutants we have made in our own life. Jesus is there all the time, while you are going through and while you are worrying God already has a plan for your escape. Even before the battle started. With wisdom comes some grief and every time God brings you out the fire the enemy is there to try to throw you right back in the fire. Even if you forget the lesson Jesus will protect you. Just think about how many times you slipped up and God picked you up? How many times you fell back into the same sin. Was defeated by the same enemy or found yourself struggling with the same battle only to find God right there. If we allow god to purify us through our mind we will remain mindful of the promises of God. The Bible reminds us of this one truth in the latter clause of 2Peter 3:1 when Paul says, "I stir up your pure minds by way of remembrance:" God will always bring us back unto subjection in order for our trials and tribulations to perfect our purpose. We forget God will take us out of ourself bring us to total subjection and reveal the call that has been put on our life. The main reason why we struggle so much as soldiers of Christ is because we are trying to fight against the General's orders. If you step back and look sometimes defeat does not come from the outside, but it comes from within. We must remember that we are Covenant people and covenant people do not give up. The heart of a stubborn and ill-minded man only delays his own destiny. When we have these urges to do things that we know are against the Word of God. When we sit and ponder and ponder and ponder trying to justify the weight behind the sin we want to commit. In our mind which is carnal we try to weigh the odds of whether or not we can sit in the house with that woman or with that man without lusting or acting unseemly. We sit in the club with the wine on the bar or that beer on our table trying to fight the weight and power of what lies in front of us- only to slip up and find out that the force that you decided to go against won and only brought you back to the alter seeking forgiveness and total subjection to the Almighty God.

In my conclusion, we see how war can have a great toll on the mind and body. We must be mentally and physically able to sustain and come out on top of all the pitfalls and setbacks of this world. We also see how Jesus attaches grace and mercy to remembrance in our everyday life to help us be victorious. When our enemy sustains every blow we have to give whatever pitfall or setback we are facing to God. Jesus is a battle ax that is a sure blow to any situation. He did it for David when he went up against Goliath. He did it for Daniel in the lion's den and He showed up for Abraham when it seemed like his only son would be the sacrifice. God has given us an advocate and the only way to prepare for the wars is to allow our advocate Jesus Christ to take our place on the battlefield and yield to the mind of the Spirit. Do not try to fight your battle alone, be reminded that the battle is not yours, but it is the Lord's. Be of good cheer, and he shall direct your path leading you to dimensions and divine destiny you never imagined. When you feel like you are going to fall, STAND. Remember, he will mount you up with wings as an eagle. Remember you have strength in Jesus not to grow weary. When it is time to stand on God's word, STAND.

He shall build his church on your steadfast heart, and the gates of Hell shall not defeat your praise. Jesus has already been where you are and has gone through every test the enemy could throw at Him. He left his victory as examples for us to follow. If we "Live on Victory's Experience" which is Jesus Christ, we will be able to say I am an overcomer and greater is He that is in me than He that is in the world. Our destiny is perfected by our warfare and purposed by God. Now raise those hands as a sign of submission to God the Father and vow to give your thoughts, problems, life, business ventures, and family troubles to Jesus Christ the Son your Advocate. Sit back, praise God for what He is about to do and watch God TKO your problems.

# CHAPTER QUESTIONS

1.  Define the Genitive Form of a word.

2.  Explain the genitive in this passage of scripture, " the weapons of our warfare are not carnal, but mighty through God to the pulling down of strong holds…"

3.  How did Solomon form a more professional army?

4.  What was the type of soldier used before Solomon formed a more professional army?

# CHAPTER 5

## Restoration

*"It is time to take back your life"*
Scripture: Job 42:10 -12

**A**nd *the LORD turned the captivity of Job, when he prayed for his friends: also the LORD gave Job twice as much as he had before. Then came there unto him all his brethren, and all his sisters, and all they that had been of his acquaintance before, and did eat bread with him in his house: and they bemoaned him, and comforted him over all the evil that the LORD had brought upon him: every man also gave him a piece of money, and every one an earring of gold. 12 So the LORD blessed the latter end of Job more than his beginning:"*

The truth hurts, it hurts so much that we tend to keep it a secret rather than expose it. The truth is so strong that it will make the strongest man weak. The truth has a lasting dictation on the mind. It will sedate the audible and confront the dishonest. It makes us face our past and force us to walk in our destiny. We all have been faced with the honesty of our over lives. We have ran and ran until what we have ran from came back into our life over and over again-You can face it, I have no doubt. Your running has created a pattern. You have the same sound of pain, the same sound of stress, and you sing the same sad song. "I will never put myself in this position again!" Restoration comes through conviction and conviction through the Word of God. Even I have been a victim of the wrath of conviction and when I allowed the restoring power of conviction to over flow my soul I felt like the greatest person on earth and knew I COULD MAKE IT. We are stuck with guilt that leaves us not wanting to look in the mirror. The hurt and the memories of our faults leave a stain on our heart. HOWEVER, His honesty and love for his people was shown by the resurrection power and the promise that "Greater works shall you [yes you] do then these." I dare you to give God PRAISE right there-Say GREATER WORKS.

There is a motto of the order of the Garter that says, "honisoit quimal y pense", which means "shame to be the person who thinks evil of it". We may have felt evil towards honesty before, I know I have. When the truth is spoken we get angry at it and storm out the church or leave our family just to avoid the pain honesty has caused us to face. Instead of believing God and trusting sincerely in him and what he has promised us we decide to clam up at the first sign of danger and run. Instead of believing God, we are not strong enough to fight for what is right. Instead we put more emphasis on where our situation has gotten us then where our situation is taking us. I was praying one day and asked God why am I always going through the same things over and over and over and over again. I asked God, "God, am I always going through, because I'm not doing it right the first time, or am I going through because there's something I need to learn?" His answer to me was, "Son, you must go through in order to break through." Sometimes we need an extra push to break through our trials. Break through the ceiling of latter purpose to get to the next level of your greater purpose. I heard someone say, you can tell a person is going through by their praise. You know when a person has a breakthrough by the extra step or the next tear in their worship. God does not allow us to suffer to be vindictive, he is not getting any joy out of our suffering, but he only gets joy out of when we endure hardness as a good soldier. When our praise is not only sincere, but honest God allows us to experience something in order to help someone else reach full conviction thus obtaining full restoration. Those mothers that are able to stay down on their knees, until someone receives their miracle. True praise elevates you to a new level in your destiny-RESTORATION. Everything that is of good news comes from God, and he will use even sometimes your enemies to give you a push. He reused that one person you laughed at or talked about, to answer a question you asked Him. God uses ordinary people to do extraordinary things; He does not always speak directly.

Watch what you say, because honesty is a reminder. When you forget what you have said honesty will be the dreadful friend to remind you. Truth will get you back to reality and thus back to God. Honesty will actually make you step out of your own life and look around and force you to see the truth through others. We all know the story of Job, we know he was going through, he could have murmured and complained, but instead Job endured every pressure that he got from his friends, wife and family. He was able to keep God first in his heart and at the end was restored to a greater purpose in God and we see Job's destiny released in his life, even after losing everything- Job was actually elevated. Most of us would have given up after the sickness, after the deaths, after losing everything. If our spouse told us to curse God and die; somebody would of did it and gave up. It is interesting how the purpose behind a simple trial only comes to elevate us to the next position in Christ. Not only do we have to surrender our will to God, but we have to be ready to be rescued from what we are going through. The one thing that restored Job, elevated Job and gave Job more than he had in the beginning. Job was honest, forthright and courageous with every answer he gave to his commentators mocking him and watching him go through his struggles. Job realized that as long as he relied on God everything was going to be alright and Job ended up getting twice the reward. Therefore, I encourage you to open up your heart to God and release your mind to His Will and this is a sign that you are ready to be rescued from the addiction of poverty thinking, debt, drugs and the regret piercing your heart everyday. Whatever you are facing; this is what God wants to see—honesty that yields submission, which produces obedience to his purpose. Hang on and I will tell you what God's true purpose for our life is. We all shall meet honesty. We all have an appointment with the truth. God says, "for I am the way, the Truth and the Life, no man cometh unto the Father except by me." We all have an appointment with truth Himself. This is an appointment we will not be late for it or have the option to reschedule. Truth will either lead you to heaven to rejoice with the Angels or lead you to suffer for eternity. Have you faced truth? If you cannot face the truth here on Earth, what makes you think when the Almighty Judge comes to tell the truth that it will set you free. Have you seen yourself? Have you examined yourself? Have you faced the truth (even though it may hurt)? Allow honesty to restore your soul. Are you ready to receive your breakthrough?

If you are tired of hiding from the truth I dare you to go to the first person, you can think of and ask them for forgiveness. Remember our conscience mind does not lie; it is linked directly to your heart, allowing true conviction to set in thus restoring us to full greatness. Whatever it is you are running from look it in the face and say, "thank you but sorry, now I must receive my breakthrough!" I dare you right where you are to SHOUT with a voice of triumph and thank God for your breakthrough! Do not let the truth crush you. Get back up and receive your heart's dreams releasing your blessing of spiritual prosperity. Our dreams and anointing are clogged by the dishonesty and lack of conviction in our life. Are you ready to be rescued? Are you ready to be restored? Remember your conviction brings change that will elevate your praise and an elevated praise will bring you to an elevated destiny. If you quit you will never experience victory.

# CHAPTER QUESTIONS

1. How is Jesus' love and honesty for us shown?

2. What is the Motto of the Order of the Garter?

3. What does the Motto of the Order of the Garter mean?

4. Why does God allow us to go through trials and experience troubles?

5. Finish this sentence, "If you_____ you will _____experience victory!

# CHAPTER 6

## Know "it" is Only a Test

*"Let God fix "it" and watch your enemies take flight "*

Scripture: Daniel 2:22

*"And he changeth the times and the seasons: he removeth kings, and setteth up kings: he giveth wisdom unto the wise, and knowledge to them that know understanding: He revealeth the deep and secret things: he knoweth what is in the darkness, and the light dwelleth with him. 23 I thank thee, and praise thee, O thou God of my fathers, who hast given me wisdom and might, and hast made known unto me now what we desired of thee: for thou hast now made known unto us the king's matter."*

The book of Daniel was written in 536 BC and was composed to give a historical account of the faithful Jews who lived in captivity. We also find in Daniel that even though in captivity God is still in control of heaven and earth. He still directs the forces of evil and good and the destiny of nations and the lives of his people. Do you know that your captivity is broken through God's sovereignty? God used man to compose this capital of books, and we know that Daniel was a young man with the personality of an elder. He was an adviser to two Babylonian kings, King Belshazzar and King Nebuchadnezzar. He was also an advisor of two middle Persian kings, King Darius and King Cyrus. Nebuchadnezzar, who was the greatest of the Babylonian kings known as a builder of cities and recognized in the Bible as one of the foreign rulers used by God for a divine purpose. Like many of us today, Nebuchadnezzar began to think of himself too highly. He began to fashion himself like a god, he was full of pride and became unteachable. Like Nebuchadnezzar we forget that the reason we are who we are and we do what we do is because God has given us the power to do it. King Nebuchadnezzar had a dream that he wanted interpreted. So he called on the magicians but they could not tell him what he wanted to know. He then called on the sorcerers and the astrologers, and they too failed the king. Despite all King Nebuchadnezzar was going to give as a reward to the one who interpreted the dream, everyone failed and was scared of the King's wrath. Because no one could fancy the king's ears he became angry and issued a decree for all the wise men to be put to death. But there were four men who had faith in the sovereign God of Israel and when Arioch, the commander of the King's guard came to where Daniel was living to complete his assignment of killing all the wise men, Daniel inquired why such a decree was made. Arioch explained to Daniel the situation and Daniel, being the man of valor he was, straightway went to the king and ask for some more time. The Scriptures says he returned home and went to his friends Hananiah, Mishael and Azariah (known to us as Shadrach, Meshach and Abendnego), so this must mean the King gave him more time or else he would have been killed right there. See sometimes our enemy has sent out a decree to destroy our destiny, but because of the gift in us our enemy's plans must change. The very person that has done you wrong, talked about you or has decreed destruction on you, recognizes keeping you around could get them to THEIR blessing-SHOUT ASSIGNMENT CANCELED!. These men Hananiah, Mishael and Azariah prayed about the problem and asked for devine intervention; God came in and answered. Daniel was able to go to King Nebuchadnezzar and reveal to the King the King's own destiny, through the King's own dream. Right here is a good place to reminisce and see God's mercy and that he will send a warning before destruction-watch and remember your dreams carefully. If God cannot get to you while you are awake He will send a dream that will cause you to "wake up" and realize life. Many have encountered sleepless nights tossing and turning our dreams causing us to wake up during the night and look around the darkroom calling on the name of Jesus; this is Jesus trying to tell you something.

Jesus will turn your circumstance around before you know it. I know sometimes it may feel like you are all alone. Nevertheless, if you look around you, you will see Jesus is in the fire with you despite how it looks. What Daniel did for the king no one else could do, but when it came down to pleasing the king again the same three Hebrew boys refused to compromise. You see, these men were friends but just because they were friends with Daniel, who found favor with the king they all had to go through a destiny shaping call to allow God to move them out of their comfort zone. Even though these gifted men were given high positions under Daniel the will of these three men not to compromise made the very person (King Nebuchadnezzar) vindictive and unpredictable. Eventhough someone may look you in your face and claim to be your bestfriend or even give you an elevation of praise I encourage you to be careful about the elevations and praises of men. The King elevated these three men, but that did not stop the king from trying to destroy them. Nebuchadnezzar was not worried about them not bowing to his graven image, but he was more concerned about the disrespect to his ego. Ego will cause the downfall of the greatest and the defeat of the strongest. This goes to show us that one day we can be the light of the world and the next day we are the target in everybody's scope of vision. What we have failed to realize being children of God is total security is in the verity that Jesus will protect us from dangers seen and unseen. Remember that if God does not okay it it will not happen-trust me.! Yes the King threw Hananiah, Mishael and Azariah in the fiery furnace to prove a point to the people, but these men still do not compromise their souls or complain. In the midst of the fire they PRAISED God and in the midst of the fire Jesus stood with them to show that he is the all sovereign God even in the fire. No matter how large we get, and no matter how puffed up our ego becomes God puts us through tests that will lead us to no other choice but to yield ourselves to Him. It is good to have some friends that are in contact with God because when times get rough you may need someone to pray for you. When you need an answer, you may need a friend to pray with you. Many times you feel all alone, left on this island of Christianity, left to survive all by yourself. You are looked at differently, coworkers do not want to come near you and nobody wants to talk to you. People that once were close to you seem far away, but my Bible tells me, that we are the salt of the Earth and we are to change the taste or ideas and actions of the world through our convicted lifestyle. You are not supposed to fit in because your difference comes from God. Now these men were connected. They knew the power of prayer and Daniel knew his life was in danger and he did not have time to fool with anyone that did not have "oil in their lamp". Anyone that could not get disconnected from the problem in order to be connected to the problem solver and Daniel did not need them around him. What he needed were some friends that were on fire for God and would not get discouraged. Daniel and these men pleaded for mercy from God concerning the mystery of King Nebuchadnezzar dream. Daniel did not want to die because of a dream that could not be interpreted. I can see these men praying all night pleading and crying out for God's mercy. They did not sit down in the time of despair, they did not complain and fight one another, but they prayed together all of them being in the same conviction came together before the throne of God. Any differences they might of had were put aside, and they came on one accord. Dear brethren in Christ, we cannot let the enemy use our situation to construct his battle plans for our lives. There is a king in each and everyone of us and we must declare that we will "write the vision and make it plain", declare that "greater is He that is within me than he that is in the world". We cannot allow him to train his foot soldiers through the lack of a prayer life or our unwillingness to allow God to restore us, to take over our life and invade our mind. We get into the habit of complaining about where we are in life. We fight with ourselves to find the answer. We shift the responsibility to someone else, and if they fail we do not try to help them out of their failure. We tell one another our problems and get mad when it surfaces around our friends and family. When it is done to us we cast down and tear down everyone and anything in our path, but this is where our problems lies. We think excessively much and pray much too little. The word of God tells us, men ought to always pray and not faint. We must pray when we feel like it and when we do not feel like it we still must pray. We must pray through our good and through our bad and even through our sisters and brothers worst times Daniel seen the need for prayer and knew he would need a little support from his brothers in order to get the task done. He did not allow his circumstance to outweigh his relationship. Yes, you went into your situation alone. Yes, it seems like no one will help you through it. Yes, you may be struggling with the sickness. The doctors have given up on you. You ask for prayer, but it seems like no one is praying, nothing is being done. You call on your friends and asked them to pray with you but they are too busy to listen. When you have the battlefield of despair looking down the barrel of your life. No family in sight for thousands and thousands of miles away. The chaplain is busy your battle buddy is sleeping. The only thing you hear is the stillness of the night. Remember, Jesus tells us that joy and peace of mind comes through him. He is telling you that as long as you depend on man you always fail and Jesus says to wait on Him, because in Him is fullness of Joy and eternal security.

This earth is not your final judgment place it is only a trial court, this is a place for all our mistakes to be made and corrected. After this life, Jesus will cross examine all of the accounts of your life. This life is the jury and you are a defendant without a lawyer and the only help to have comes from the judge. Jesus has given us a path of justice and we must follow his path. Our trial would lead to a not guilty verdict, but if we compromise and misjudge the security that is in Jesus we will be found guilty of the ultimate crime. That is a crime of sin. This trial court will takes us through cross-examine after cross-examine and trial after trial, but the end is what counts. Just like in the world, the trial is not more important than the verdict. The verdict is the sentence and the outcome may have you calling for a retrial or an appeal. At the end of this sovereign judgment is not going to be a retrial or any appeals. However, after the verdict will be your sentencing. In our text the three Hebrew boys did not have a trial they had a verdict and then they we sentenced and thrown in the fiery furnace. Nevertheless, Jesus still had the last word.

If you are worrying about pleasing this world do not waste your time; we will never be able to please the world. This flesh is never satisfied. It is always crying for more. We need to worry about making Jesus happy. He is the one that puts us through and goes through with us. Your friends and family will put you through and leave you there, you will try your best to please the world, but the world will always do its best to be unhappy. You tried to do what people say will be the best for you, but when you do it they want to question your love for them but remember our lives are wrapped in the security and sovereignty of God. The only sense of comfort, you will ever have in Jesus. No man lay down his life and had power to pick it up again but Jesus. Leave your problems to Him and place your security in His sovereignty. The only sense of comfort you will ever have is in God knowing that he sees your pain, and he says He has already made a way for you to escape. He is true, hold on and be of good courage, and he shall direct your path. God is the light for our feet when the way is too dark to see, Jesus is the way the truth and the life. No one comes to the Father but by Him. This is your trial, what will your verdict be? Would it be guilty Or not guilty? Are you waiting to hear the King say you may enter into eternal rest or are you afraid you may hear depart from me ye worker of iniquity I never knew you? *"I thank thee, and praise thee, O thou God of my fathers, who hast given me wisdom and might, and hast made known unto me now what we desired of thee: for thou hast now made known unto us the king's matter."* My friend when it seems like your prayers have vanished and life has come after you unjustly, just know that where you are is a trial and Jesus have already declared you NOT GUILTY. So take back your place in the ranks of the Lord's Army and resume command over your life—let the Devil know, I AM SECURE!

# CHAPTER QUESTIONS

1. According to Job 42:10-12 God turned Job's captivity around because of what?

2. What year was the Book of Daniel written?

3. Why was the Book of Daniel written?

4. If a person gets caught up in "ego" what can and will happen to that person? How do we avoid this tragedy from happening to us?

5. Hananiah, Mishael and Azariah are the Hebrew names for whom?

# Chapter 7

*Keep the Volume Up*

*"Everyone has Growing Pains"*

Scripture: Ephesians 4:13

"**T**ill we all come in the unity of the faith, and of the knowledge of the Son of God, unto a perfect man, unto the measure of the stature of the fullness of Christ:"

In the book of Ephesians the writer Paul is talking to the believers, the set body of people that have accepted Jesus Christ as their Lord and Savior. He is writing to strengthen them and to explain the purpose of the church in the body of Christ in their life. Paul did not just write to them without knowing who they were, but he actually spent time with them (a total of three years to be exact). He spent time with the elders of the church, and grew very close to them that even though the church at Ephesus was close to such a powerful and gifted man of God like Paul, they still had to seek God for themselves. Many times we think that since we are connected with a powerful source that we do not need to be connected to God for ourselves. We must understand to get to know the man we need to know and live his plan. Life will not be easy when we fully give our life to God. When you leave the world totally behind and allow God to transform your mind you will realize more situations, more tests, more trials and more discomforts will arise in your life. People who use to talk to you will not want to talk to you anymore, they may even tell you, "Go ahead try that Jesus thing we will see you back out here with us soon"- KEEP THE VOLUME UP! People that used to understand you will some way or another not understand you anymore-KEEP THE VOLUME UP! In addition, when it seems like you have gotten past the one discomforts, the one lie, the one disappointment there is always another one waiting for you on the next level-KEEP THE VOLUME UP. What we need to understand is when we tell God, we want to be more like him, He will allow us to do just that. We must live out that prayer and begin to really live like Christ. Jesus was crucified for doing the work of the Father he had to sustain some scars mentally and physically. He had to have proof to prove he gave. So when we think on what he did for us we remember the nailed scarred hands, His feet nailed together, a crown of thorns on His head, piercings in his side, mocking, the spitting upon, the cries of the people, the prayers of the saints around Him and the convictions of those crucifying him this is what we should think about when our trials come to disturb us. Jesus gave his complete all that our purpose may be obtained and our destinies to stand up. Jesus did not come so that we would be comfortable with the world but he came that the world and those that serve him would have a difference between them. However, this conflict is not designed to disturb you, but this conflict has been corroded by the enemy to try and distress your destiny from speaking to your purpose so that you may be all that God has called you to be. The Bible says grieve not the Holy Spirit. Therefore, the Holy Spirit does not come to grieve us, but it comes to satisfy us and comes to push us into the abundant life. Nevertheless, when we allow growing pains to influence our mind to believe that we are abnormal, we will always be in an abnormal place in our mind; this is one place the enemy comes to disturb our thinking to block your kingdom expansion. Growing pains do not come unless we grow or are growing at a constant rate. If we are not growing or if our growth is diminutive then the pains will not be there or they will not be so intense to where they cause us discomfort. If you are not feeling some kind of pressure from the world, or pressure from your destiny pushing you away from the ordinary to "pressure" you into the extraordinary it is fair to say that we have not matured in the statutes of God's promises. How many of us can say that we have given our complete all? How many people can look back over and over their life and remember the scars, remember the lies? How many people have change their identity to the point where people knew your name, but do not recognize you because grace has overshadowed your face? How many really feel the life of Jesus beginning to work for them and through them? To be the body of Christ we must first suffer. We as a people learn better when we are actively taking part in learning the scriptures and life of Jesus. When we have a hands-on experience we tend to grasp the concept a little better. The word of God says until we all come in the unity of the faith and of the knowledge of the son of God, but how are we supposed to come into the unity of the son of God, and obtained the unity or completeness of his knowledge when we do not take a hands-on approach and experience first-hand the true life of Jesus? It may hurt sometimes to have people call you a liar. It may hurt to have people cast you aside, it may hurt to be in debt and see no way through. It may hurt to lose a loved one, it may hurt, but it is for our perfection. To be perfect we have to let the Father take out our imperfections and through His cleaning power we will witness the healing of old scars and old relationships. Some things will leave your mind bemused and leave you wondering if this is how your life will always be-Point to yourself and say "It is only growing pains!" Jesus is trying to mature us and to be mature means to let some things in our life go that are keeping us from the fullness of Christ Jesus. You have to let them go. I need you to get this point right here; Jesus paid it all and we have been reconciled, through Jesus, into a new family, so when we were reconciled we were brought into a new society, with a new identity. We were united with our father that we once were separated from by sin. Sin caused us at birth to be separated from God the father, but when we were born again, through Jesus Christ the Son, we were brought into a new family, evidence through the redemptive power of the blood of Jesus sealed by the renewing authority through the baptism of the Holy Spirit. So we were taking from the hands of death handed back into the hands of Life-God the Father. Remember Jesus said he is the way the truth and the life and no man cometh unto the Father (God) unless they go through his process-we must go through Jesus Christ the Son in order to get to the ordained purpose of God for our life. Next time someone asks you, what is wrong, just tell them "Man it is only Growing Pains". So why do we not believe in Isaiah 40:31? Jesus said all we have to do is wait and he will renew our strength. So when you get tired of the same arguments, the same let downs and the same life routines KEEP THE PRAISE VOLUME UP. When trials and tribulations come PUSH the VOLUME of your PRAISE to another LEVEL-Praise harder and worry less. Let God give you strength to get through it and pull through the other side of quit- Which is victory through Jesus Christ. If we give our problems over to the Lord, we do not have to worry about the growing pains of weakness that we experience in the time of our troubles. If God in Isaiah 41 took heed to everyone's life, he expects us to take heed to the life, the legacy and the example that Jesus left for us. He says if the poor and the needy seek water we must nourish them. If there is no one there to unpack the overcrowded gateway of their heart, we are suppose to be there to pry them doors open with our love. So come into your blessing today, and seek those things that are spiritual and those things that are divine and endure the pains of growing for those pains only come from purpose pushing destiny into position. Be, say and do all you can through Christ Jesus today.

# CHAPTER QUESTIONS

1. Who is Paul writing to in the Book of Ephesians?


2. Why did Paul even write the Book of Ephesians?
3. What is the title of this Chapter?


4. In your present situation name 5 ways you can get through life's "Growing Pains".

# Chapter 8

## Identify Relationships Blocking Destiny

*"Is it a love, lust or crush relationship?"*

Scripture: John 3:16-17

"For God so loved the world, that he gave his only begotten Son, that whosoever believeth in him should not perish, but have everlasting life. For God sent not his Son into the world to condemn the world; but that the world through him might be saved".

We must first get a better understanding of the meanings of love, lust and crush. Webster defines love as a strong tender affection or a deep devotion. Lust is defined as a strong craving or a strong desire. A crush is defined as to become broken in shape or pressured; to oppress. Love is a little word, but has great meaning. Love must be something that is not forced or influenced by the wrong reasons. We as a people have altered the true meaning of love. We are comfortable with one night stands, no strings attached, and an attitude that is pleased with "as long as she ain't pregnant" mentalities that have created more broken homes, single mother parents and unnecessary stress on our destinies. God gave the ultimate example of love when he gave his only Begotten Son for people not worthy of God's "thought power"-never mind His son. God wants us to come to a realization that without him love is not truly love; and without true love the destiny awaiting you is unreachable.

There is a relationship between fear and love. In Exodus 20:20 Moses speaks to the people letting them know that God does not want them to be scared of him but he was showing his power only to prove that he was the Almighty God. When you are all alone and feel like escaping out of the box religion seems to have you in the respective fear you have for God, knowing he is the Almighty is what keeps you steadfast. Understanding that God's almighty power has the ability to release your destiny to walk with your purpose and focus not on our self but on kingdom principles of Spiritual Prosperity. Through this type of relationship with God, we will think twice about stepping out of line, giving up, and giving in to relationships that do not reverence the places God would want us to go in life. Fear is an emotion, it is not something given to you, but it is caused by danger, evil thoughts and feelings of pain, or misguided judgments that cause erroneous destinies and confusing delays in our life. The fear of God is the pain of your prayers being unheard, but the peace of God is to know that evil cannot and will not harm you and that God will unite relationships to agree with your calling and destiny in life. When you are in the ark of safety and see evil all around you, fear comes in when you realize that "if I fall out of the ark" I will be swallowed up by the despair and desolation God has been protecting me from; watch the company you keep- relationships can modify your destiny and change the outcome of your season. Here is where the uneasiness steps in and says "God is not here now", who will protect me from me? Who will stop me from destroying my finances and complicating God's plan for my life-yes we can complicate God's plan by not yielding to His guidance and understanding. If we rather have a relationship with the world and only care about what we think the world can do for us, our peace of mind will be in the hands of the world and not in the arms of the Father. So if we rely on the world system to guide us, what happens when peace is gone and war is all around us? What happens when the economy falls and depression sets in? The world is unstable, the only stability we have is the sure foundation of

God the Father that provided calmness to the sea by speaking a prophetic word. God can provide this same comfort and serenity to our life if we just allow Him to speak a word to our destiny and live according to His purpose. When we have a true Christian relationship that is not influenced by love according to this world we can make a difference. When we do not confuse true love with lust in our heart then our thinking can be changed and our season planted for blessings to be harvested. When you are nailed hands and feet to your situation, and it feels like a bed of thorns piercing your heart, remember Jesus. When the devil has you battling with your flesh ask yourself "Did I give the Devil permission to attack me through the compromises in my life?" Romans 8:17 says "And if children, then heirs; heirs of God and joint heirs with Christ; if so be that we suffer with him, that we may be also glorified together". Paul is using adoption in this passage. In the Bible days there were two words used to describe a son; Teknon , which is son by birth and Hious meaning son by character change or adoption. Paul in Romans 8:17 is telling us that if we are children, we are inheritors of Christ, and if we are inheritors of Christ and share in his suffering we will through our suffering share, in his glory. This straight and narrow way is not easy, but it is possible. This life is not just based on lusting or having some silly crush, but there needs to be some evidence of love somewhere. When you are adopted you gain full rights into the new family. You no longer participate in the things of the old family but walk and live in the things of the new family. That goes for us as Christians we are to be Christ like. I heard someone say that they do not like being called a Christian-they do not like that word. Well when we are converted from a Teknon to a Hious state of kinship, we have no other choice but to be a Christian. When God saves us we inherit His family and all the benefits that come with being His child. The word of God in 2 Corinthians 5:17 replies to your Godly agreement like this, "Therefore if any man *be* in Christ, *he is* a new creature: old things are passed away; behold, all things are become new". Here we witness a prophetic utterance from God to remind us that "if any man" be in Christ the old things we did and the old ways we thought have to become new. The phrase "if any man" is the Indefinite Pronoun that does not refer to any specific person or persons, but relates to all mankind (women, men, children, boys and girls). Therefore, there is no way an adopted child of the Father can still have the mind of a Hious kinship. Yes, we were born in sin: this is the identity of a man born by birth. However, when we have been born again we become a son by character change and no longer accept the identity neither the destiny we were born with-We we are changed we must also change our thinking. Now, we believe in a greater love that is better than one night stands and quick blessings that only last until the next good talent or favor comes along. Do not sale your blessing for recognition from the world or an elevation of temporary success. Do not allow the favors that "man" can through at you to dictate your blessing-do not take from the hands of the world or else the world will hold the fate of your destiny in their hand. Instead, take from the hands of God, for his plan for your life is not determined by favors, but determined through Favor. According to John 13:27-28 my Bible tells me that God loves us in spite of what He knows about us and since God knows all that is a lot of love for a world that refuses to know the Lord in the suffering of His death and the glory of His ressurection. True love will love you despite what they know about you. If anyone truly loves you, they would forget the past, forgive and encourage you along the way.

There is a difference between being in love with someone and just loving someone. See genuine love is love that does not quit. Despite all our accounts that are in debt with Christ Jesus He still heals us, delivers us, forgives us and loves us unconditionally. This is because Jesus is in love with us. When someone "just loves you", that kind of love can run dry, because it is influenced by the wrong spirit. Love grows on a person, which is why the question always comes to mind when dealing with couples "Do you love them or are you in love with them?" Is there a time when a true Christian relationship needs outside influences to help someone realize they love someone? Love is supposed to be genuine and not shaken down. True Christians have the true love of the father in them. This is where we must differentiate between love, lust or a crush. The Bible tells me. Love is patient so lust must require immediate attention. Lust tells your mind that your body needs it now despite the illegality or immoralities behind satisfying your craving. The Word of God also tells us love is kind, so lust has to be harsh, rude; bad-mannered and ill-tempered by nature. If you need to force your love physically, mentally or emotionally on anything or anyone then your love is not genuine. Love does not demand to have its own way it has patience and allows time to construct the way; waiting for destiny and purpose to collide. The devil is slick he will make our lust feel like love, but when you give in to this lust it results in unyielding and unguided self-disgust and hatred. If you cannot wait, what you feel is not true and you need to search yourself and analyze the influences around you making you fell this way.

The characteristics of true love according to 1 Corinthians13:4-7 are these things: Charity suffereth long, *and* is kind; charity envieth not; charity vaunteth not itself, is not puffed up, Doth not behave itself unseemly, seeketh not her own, is not easily provoked, thinketh no evil; Rejoiceth not in iniquity, but rejoiceth in the truth; Beareth all things, believeth all things, hopeth all things, endureth all things." According to Corinthians, charity cannot be some fly by night emotion. It has to be something genuine and firm; rooted and ingrained in truth to bear all, believe all and hope in all (this is faith in action). If you have faith in the love you have for your business, career, or life success and no faith in the Kingdom of God and seek not its righteousness to have all these things added unto you, then you have a commitment of love versus an understanding of love. When you are working in true love, you will not have to talk about it or puff it up. Matthew 9:5 tells me the difference between talking about love versus demonstrating it is when Jesus ask the question "For whether is easier, to say, *Thy* sins be forgiven thee; or to say, Arise, and walk?" Jesus goes on to say in verse 6, "But that ye may know that the Son of man hath power on earth to forgive sins…." It is one thing to hear of God's power but it is another thing to see God's power in action. There is something about the demonstration of love that overrides the talk about love. If you are going to do something, do not talk about it be about it, go towards the goal stop talking about the goal of true faith. God blesses a working destiny.

True love recognizes the legal, moral and self rights of others. Love is to be displayed if you feel like giving it or not. Love is not just a physical emotion displayed by the union of husband and wife but love according to the Book of James, "loves thy neighbor as you love thyself." We do not love ourselves for a day or for just a few minutes. We do not love ourselves until the lust has ran out. We do not say we love ourselves and after demonstration (or physical activity) of our love is demonstrated our feelings turn into hatred. Do not force yourself to love anything or anyone because we do not force ourselves to love ourselves. We are born to love ourselves so it should be this way for whatever we pursue. Dreams are birthed by a vision resulting in our destiny birthed by love, trust and acceptance in God. I have told you what Paul, Matthew and other great men have said about love. However, what does God have to say? God says that he so loved the world that he gave his only begotten son that who so ever believed on him shall not perish but have everlasting life. Not only is this love, but it is a promise. A promise that God's love would guide us and plan our destiny for us. You do not have to worry about the money; just worry about the Kingdom. God says since he loves us we are to depend and lean on his every word, not only lean, but trust also in every word breathed by God. Jesus gave us the ultimate example of love when he died on the cross. Jesus gave us the ultimate example of perseverance, purpose being released into destiny, the true meaning of Spiritual Prosperity is when Jesus walked to the place designed for His crucifixion, and their He sacrificed His life for us. Jesus did not need exaltations from man to prove that His destiny would come alive through God's purpose for His life and neither do you. Matthew 23:6 tells us not to be worried about selfish recognition. Luke 16 tells us not to worry about earthly belongings, but only worry about the love extend to us by God required to be extended to everyone you come in contact with. God does not want us to lust after our destiny, but he wants us to have patience and understanding that he will find the path of genuine love that will lead us into our purpose. This love will fulfill the law of love and man. When we do not settle for quick unyielding satisfactions, but truly find something we love, cherish and enjoy then and only then will our endeavors not block our destiny. Remember that love is J.E.S.U.S (Just Enough Shed Under Salvation).

# CHAPTER QUESTIONS

1. Fear is an emotion not given to us by God, so if fear is in our life who is behind this emotion?

2. Now that we know who is behind fear, how are we to deal with it?

3. What are the characteristics of TRUE love according to 1 Corinthians 13:4-7?

4. In 1 Corinthians 13:4-7, what does the word *charity* mean?

5. The author gave you a phrase at the end of the chapter. What does each letter stand for in J.E.S.U.S?

# Chapter 9

## Recognize Compromise

### *"Do not compromise to be Recognized"*
Scripture: Genesis 3:1-10

*Now the serpent was more subtil than any beast of the field which the LORD God had made. And he said unto the woman, Yea, hath God said, Ye shall not eat of every tree of the garden? And the woman said unto the serpent, We may eat of the fruit of the trees of the garden: But of the fruit of the tree which is in the midst of the garden, God hath said, Ye shall not eat of it, neither shall ye touch it, lest ye die. And the serpent said unto the woman, Ye shall not surely die: For God doth know that in the day ye eat thereof, then your eyes shall be opened, and ye shall be as gods, knowing good and evil.*

*And when the woman saw that the tree was good for food, and that it was pleasant to the eyes, and a tree to be desired to make one wise, she took of the fruit thereof, and did eat, and gave also unto her husband with her; and he did eat. And the eyes of them both were opened, and they knew that they were naked; and they sewed fig leaves together, and made themselves apron. And they heard the voice of the LORD God walking in the garden in the cool of the day: and Adam and his wife hid themselves from the presence of the LORD God amongst the trees of the garden.*

*And the LORD God called unto Adam, and said unto him, Where art thou? And he said, I heard thy voice in the garden, and I was afraid, because I was naked; and I hid myself.*

Before we get to this truth and how God will use your conviction to enhance your destiny. You must first look at Genesis chapter 2, and read about how God made the earth and how beautiful it was. How he made man and set him in the garden we know by the name of Eden. In the Garden of Eden was everything man needed, desired and wished for. The interesting thing about the Garden of Eden is the fact that man was made after the garden. Therefore we can conclude that the Garden of Eden in its splendor and pleasure and its grandeur was designed for man's purpose. The Bible tells us "And the Lord God planted a garden eastward in Eden; and there he put the man whom he had formed."In the beginning God made sure that we were set and would not have to worry about anything. God did not make man then have a man plant the garden, but he made the earth, then made the garden and then had man tend to the garden that was made for him. This shows us that God not only allows us to enjoy some things that he has made for us, but in order to enjoy these things we must tend to them to make us more grateful we have received blessings from God. In order for your purpose to release into your destiny you must first understand how to take care of what God has given you and be happy in the position he has placed you in before He can elevate you. Say to yourself, "SELF, I must appreciate to elevate!" In the garden was beauty for the eyes of man, and it pleased God to see his creation in its splendor and happiness. Also in this garden was a tree called the tree of knowledge of good and evil. If man was to eat of it they would recognize sin and recognize good from evil. Even to this day this Tree of Knowledge of Good and Evil is present in us (if you do not believe me watch how a child acts when they do something wrong). It is so prevalent that we are born into sin. But we will not stop compromising the destiny that God has planned for us by recognizing the temporary destiny the enemy has brought before us. See, it was the enemy that caused the minds of man to compromise and eat the fruit of the forbidden tree. For in their mind they could not understand how God will find out that they had tasted of the fruit. Along with their disbelief came unbelief in the power God has and His omniscient presence-they allowed a compromise to amend good judgment and caused the entire destiny of the human race to be transformed-But all things work out for the good of those that love God and are called according to [what] HIS PURPOSE. Now we are held prisoners to sin and the only way to be made free is to confess those sins, repent (turn away from our wicked ways) and accept Jesus Christ as our personal Savior and then watch how the scripture will be fulfilled in your life as God prepares you for the baptism of the Holy Ghost with fire and power. We drop our sins, but pick up a compromise. Compromise is slowly creeping into the church and the lies of the enemy are trying to alter the standards of salvation from that of holiness to that of "come as you are and do as you please" religions. I beseech you brethren, do not (I repeat) do not allow the enemy to lower the standards of the Church. For in these standards God has given purpose and is trying to release the Church into a higher blessing then what we can see. In your situation do not try to think your way out but instead allow God to show you the way out. Stay in the fire and let God make you pure as gold worth of reward. Do not let the enemy take over your mind but allow God to transform the renewing of your mind and make you think like His son. You cannot continue to make compromises and expect promises in your life to come true, but in order to see the promises come to light you must recognize all compromise and glorify God and push toward the promise. For the promise does not come in lowering the standards or giving in to the fruits of the enemy. The enemy's promises are lies and disappointments, but every promise of God is yeah and amen and come by pulling down every stronghold in our life. Recognize the compromise. Do not believe for one minute that God does not mind compromise in order to gain a temporary purpose. Be not deceived God is not mocked, whatever a man soweth that is what he shall reap. If you sow bountifully then you shall reap a bountiful harvests but if you sow sparingly you will reap a sparing harvest. If you want your purpose to be bountiful then sow a bountiful life. If you read the accounts of the Bible God is telling us he knows the intent of our heart. Moreover, we are so negligent that we do not see his word is alive. God is telling us that we will compromise our destiny if we do not allow Him to prove His purpose. Just as he did with Job He is doing the same thing with us. We go to work trying to fit in with friends compromising everything we stand for the recognition. Friends not knowing that you have been born again unless you tell them. Business partners do not know you work on faith and rely on God to get your deal after deal. What are we ashamed of? If the world can boast about their parties, one night stands, shout out curse words in our presence and blatantly disrespect or denounce God in our presence, why are we ashamed to live the life of a Christian or testify about God's goodness, longsuffering and saving power? Taking all the credit when we know that all our works is orchestrated by God. Woman of God dressing like the world is compromise. All of the compromise we encounter in life distorts and changes our purpose. The great thing about God is that destiny is never altered. God will allow us to veer off only to make us realize that we must get back on track but compromise makes her time in the desert longer. God is not pleased with compromise; he has mapped out the destiny that wants to meet up with your purpose in life.

God has instructed me to tell you we are getting too "smart" for own good and too relaxed to see the danger approaching us. If America continues to decide to find the middle ground and compromise the very Godly principles and ethics we were founded on, destruction is coming soon-America must continue to take the higher ground and neither negotiate or compromise with the antagonistic views of the Devil's purpose. I'm here to tell you if we do not know that the enemy has a destiny he wants us to do we are sadly mistaken. The only way the Adversary's plan can work is if we continue to purpose in our hearts to let that plan work. God is faithful and just to forgive us from all of our sins and cleanses us from all the unrighteousness and defeat all antagonistic thoughts and lead us to the path of Divine Purpose leading us to a greater Destiny. Are you giving God your full potential or are you giving him half of what you really can do?

When a Christian and the unbeliever are standing next to one another and you cannot tell the difference between them does this please God? There is to be a difference between light and dark; evil and good. Along with this difference there is supposed to be a recognizable change. We must not allow the church to continue looking like the world and the world being the influence on the church instead of the church being the influence on the world. Unbelievers do not want anything to do with the church because the church has too many commonalities with the world. Just because God is invisible to our natural does not mean he is impossible-Just because we cannot see God like we see ourselves does not mean salvation is not real and just because God is invincible does not mean he does not see what we are doing or not doing. Just because your eyes have not seen or looked upon him does not mean he does not record every detail of your compromise throughout life. This brings me to a question. Just because we have not seen Hell does this mean that Hell is not real? When you get to the revelation of whether or not Hell is real tell yourself, "If hell is real then faith must be real and if faith is real God is real and Heaven has really been prepared for me." See we live every day by faith and without faith we would not be able to make it but when we want something from God we must bring our faith the size of a mustard seed to get receive from Him. What we have to remember is that God is the way the truth and the life he is Lord of lords King of kings Alpha and Omega the author and finisher because he made us and he will deliver us. God has no respect of person and He has no respect of sin either. There is no such thing as a white lie or I will do this one time God will understand. Remember God sees every sin and every compromise. It is bad to compromise your salvation and take part in things you know God is against. A compromise is something you do that is out of the normal in order to be accepted. Some people compromise for personal gain but the Saints of God are called to be different. We must separate ourselves whether it is personal business or family business we must not allow the enemy to deceive us into compromising but take a stand on the truth of holiness and stop compromising destiny to be accepted by the world. When we compromise we allow faith to be taken away and fear to set in. The enemy is always busy and if he can get us to lower our standard he can also lower your threshold to recognize compromise; this is why we have some people in the church that cannot receive a breakthrough this is why there are so many problems hounding the homes minds and bodies of the Saints and why we get confused about our purpose in life. I have come to tell you there is only one purpose, but many destines in life-the purpose of God. If the enemy can get you to adjust your morals, if he can get you to shift your thoughts and have you accept that you are doing the wrong thing when all along you are doing the right thing compromise will set in. Some might tell you that there is no such thing as the Trinity, but I am here to tell you today that God is the Father, Jesus is the Son sitting on the right hand of the Father and the Holy Ghost is the power to avoid compromise and the key to reaching your destiny. There is only one name given unto men whereby we must be saved and at the Name of Jesus every knee shall bow and every tongue confess that Jesus is Lord. Are you battling with your own demons, addictions or is your past preventing you from excelling-I dare you to shout JESUS! See if the adversary can attack your mind on your lowest level, he will slowly eat away at you and pretty soon your compromise will have you bound and not know what to do to get out of this bound state. A saint that compromises to be recognized is dangerous. They are dangerous to their destiny, to God's purpose, to their called and to themselves-do not sell yourself short for an overnight recognition.

Our blessing is in the Word not in the world. Man cannot deliver you, the world cannot set you free, but God will make your name great and make it so every person in this nation will see who you are, what you have become and what God will help you do next. Greatness is in the heart and mind of every believer. No matter how old you get or how young or old some may think you are remember greatness is the destiny of every blood washed believer. God wants us to prosper as our soul doeth prosper. Spiritual prosperity comes before earthly prosperity; this is the order of Divine Destiny (Matthew 6:33, Seek ye first the Kingdom of God and everything you have dreamed of and wished for will be given to you). When the world has given you all of their praise and have ran out of good things to say about Jesus is there to pick you up and exchange your depression for His blessings and old impressions of you for lasting impressions of you. We want God to bless us and prosper our lives but we do not have any strength when it comes to the desires of our flesh. The word of truth and the word of faith in the Gospel truth has been distorted to fit the desires, the mold of negative thinking and dislikes of unbelievers. When you disobey you are disregarding the rule that God has placed over you ordained and sanctioned by the very Will of God. This is where compromising will come in and confuses your destiny. When it comes down to worldly of fleshly things we tend to give in so easily and lower our standards and say we will do better next time. Compromise is how America has ended up as a Nation stained with so many scandals and corporate and political disappointments. Dating back to the Garden of Eden and the days Abraham, Isaac and Jacob we can find evidence of compromise and the contentment of living in a world crimsoned with iniquity and disobedience. We are taking grace for granted and soon mercy is going to run faint with the compromise of our life. Why do you think it feels like when you try to praise the Lord your hands are weighed down or when you try to worship it feels like your worship is unheard and your prayers are ineffective? If you try the way of Jesus without the compromise may be our relationship with God will be like our forefathers in the gospel. Maybe without compromise you will be able to heal the sick, raise the dead, open the eyes of the blinded man; this will all come from not compromise. No compromise will put you in the right place at the right time for a blessing. Without compromise we would be able to run organizations without them failing because of financial corruption and high-level controversy. The source of a good business comes from the fruit of a good source-not compromising will put you in the right place at the right time for a blessing. We can start by saying Lord forgave me from all inconsistencies, compromise and down falls that I have committed. Pray this prayer, "God cleanse my mind and purge me from the thoughts of compromise. Release my destiny O' Lord and take me into the realm of the inner Court of your purpose over my life. Lord I repent from my distorted thinking and ask for the path to be revealed unto me again- I want to get back the vision you gave me for my life; release it now God. Please release it now in the Name of Jesus, Amen. It is done, now praise the Lord for bringing you out and setting you free. Do not compromise to be recognized, but recognize the compromise.

# CHAPTER QUESTIONS

1. According to scripture was what the serpent told Eve the exact words told to Adam by God? What does this teach us?

2. Was Adam created before the Garden of Eden or was the Garden of Eden created before Adam? Why?

3. Where is greatness found in a believer?

4. The author talks about Divine Destiny. What is Divine Destiny?

5. What is the Order of Divine Destiny and what scripture explains this truth?

# Chapter 10

## *Life Application Chapter*

Understanding God's purpose allows us to let him guide our destiny. We all want to know what our purpose in life is to be I encourage everyone to listen to destiny's voice as she speaks to you through the word of God. It is easy to apply the truths that we went over today: understand God's power, believe it, achieve it, survive the storm, L.O.V.E, restoration, know that "it" is a test, keep the volume up, identify relationships block your destiny and recognize compromise. My brothers and my dear sisters I beseech you to take time out to meditate on where you are in life take time to analyze what you are thinking and whether or not what you are thinking, living and pursuing is going to make you happy. If the people of America would try love, peace and happiness instead of hatred, complaining and compromise our generation would not be the way it is today. Young people understand that you raise your family and what you teach them is influenced by what they see. This generation has been polluted by the idea of sex, drugs, violence, single-parent homes and many more things is the status quo and the way to reach prosperity and destiny. We have live with it but we do not have to accept it. Jesus is looking for a few good men and that includes a few good women too willing to stand up and declare the works of the Lord as the status quo. We are not to lower our standards but understand God's purpose for our life. Go the extra mile to witness salvation to someone. Remember if it is wrong it is wrong and if it's time to stop its time to put it down. See for yourself this mortal body is never pleased. Allow God to show you that flesh always wants more. The only way that we can over ride the failures in life is by hope and prayer believing in God to show us the way through. Do not adapt to the world's system of thinking, but overcome by the spirit of prayer fasting and continuing to believe in the word of God-this is how we survived the storm. If we allow ourselves to govern our own lives we will lose what God has ordained for us. Visions are not the same and anointing are not the same anymore because we have misplaced our understanding of the Deity of Christ and the power of his restoration. We have to cry out to God in order to reach truth number five, restoration. God is worthy of all the praise glory and honor and worship God through the restoration that he has left for us. Through praise comes the passing of every test; for there is victory in praise. Know that what you are going through is only a test to make you prepared for where God is taking you. Do not let situations disturb you but allow God to disturb the situation. 2 Chronicles 7:8-12 reminds us to make preparations for a destination, but in order for our destination to be prepared we must first identify relationships blocking this destiny.

The burden has been lifted by the weight of our praise. The process of deliverance has been completed through our worship. Continue to use praise to press out every imperfection and leave it to God to figure out the rest. Hang your burden upon the cloud of Shekinah glory and allow God to cover your situation. My pastor Bishop Mark Walden once said "pray until you pray through!" In his words of wisdom I encourage you to pray without ceasing-Whatever you do do not stop. With Kingdom thinking you can take back your Kingdom blessing predestined to you from God and taken from you by the enemy and kept from your eyes by your own misunderstanding. If you change the way you think you can change your life and the life of people around you but the only way to do this is to focus on our last truth, truth #9. We must recognize every compromise in our life and stop lowering our standards to be recognized by the world for only a season. Holiness is a term used to describe a separation or a people set apart for the purpose of God. There are some things that holy people and the world will not see the same but this is okay. We all want to know what our purpose is in life, but I challenge you to leave the purpose to God and pray for God to revel to you your destiny. If we look at Job 1 we can see that the purpose of our warfare is not flesh and blood and every test and trial is purposed by God. God has called on us to prove to Satan and the world that He (God that is) still has a holy nation willing to stand on His Word and praise His name despite what they are going through. He has called on us to prove that holiness is still right and salvation is still available to them that believe. Our destiny is to fulfill this purpose in God and our destiny benefits us through spiritual prosperity and abundant living through the precious blood of Jesus Christ. Remember to reach this level of prosperity we must understand God's Power, Believe it, Achieve it, do your best to survive the storm, L.O.V.E (Live on Victory's Experience), seek for total restoration, Know that what you are going through "it" is only a test, Keep the Volume Up, Identify Relationships Blocking Your Destiny and whatever you do Recognize Compromise. In the glory of our Father and the peace of Jesus Christ the Son, I encourage you to continue to LOVE (Live On Victory's Experience) and SMILE (Show More Inducing Love Everyday).

# REFERENCES

*The Holy Bible : King James Version.* 1995 (electronic ed. of the 1769 edition of the 1611 Authorized Version.) (Mt 21:23-27). Bellingham WA: Logos Research Systems, Inc.

[2]Wood, D. R. W., & Marshall, I. H. (1996). *New Bible dictionary* (3rd ed.) (945). Leicester, England; Downers Grove, Ill.: InterVarsity Press.

[3]*The Holy Bible : King James Version.* 1995 (electronic ed. of the 1769 edition of the 1611 Authorized Version.) (Heb 11:1-3). Bellingham WA: Logos Research Systems, Inc.

[4]*The Holy Bible : King James Version.* 1995 (electronic ed. of the 1769 edition of the 1611 Authorized Version.) (1 Co 8:6-7). Bellingham WA: Logos Research Systems, Inc.

[5]*The Holy Bible : King James Version.* 1995 (electronic ed. of the 1769 edition of the 1611 Authorized Version.) (Is 12:2-6). Bellingham WA: Logos Research Systems, Inc.

[6]*The Holy Bible : King James Version.* 1995 (electronic ed. of the 1769 edition of the 1611 Authorized Version.) (Mt 8:23-27). Bellingham WA: Logos Research Systems, Inc.

[7]*The Holy Bible : King James Version.* 1995 (electronic ed. of the 1769 edition of the 1611 Authorized Version.) (2 Co 10:1-5). Bellingham WA: Logos Research Systems, Inc

[8]*The Holy Bible : King James Version.* 1995 (electronic ed. of the 1769 edition of the 1611 Authorized Version.) (Job 42:10-12). Bellingham WA: Logos Research Systems, Inc.

[9]*The Holy Bible : King James Version.* 1995 (electronic ed. of the 1769 edition of the 1611 Authorized Version.) (Da 2:21-23). Bellingham WA: Logos Research Systems, Inc.

[10]*The Holy Bible : King James Version.* 1995 (electronic ed. of the 1769 edition of the 1611 Authorized Version.) (Jn 3:16-17). Bellingham WA: Logos Research Systems, Inc.

[11]*The Holy Bible : King James Version.* 1995 (electronic ed. of the 1769 edition of the 1611 Authorized Version.) (2 Co 5:17). Bellingham WA: Logos Research Systems, Inc.

[12]*The Holy Bible : King James Version.* 1995 (electronic ed. of the 1769 edition of the 1611 Authorized Version.) (1 Co 13:4-7). Bellingham WA: Logos Research Systems, Inc.

[13]*The Holy Bible : King James Version.* 1995 (electronic ed. of the 1769 edition of the 1611 Authorized Version.) (Mt 9:5). Bellingham WA: Logos Research Systems, Inc.

[14]*The Holy Bible : King James Version.* 1995 (electronic ed. of the 1769 edition of the 1611 Authorized Version.) (Ge 3:1-10). Bellingham WA: Logos Research Systems, Inc.

[15] Definition of **Indefinite Pronoun** (page 52). Zodhiates, S., & Baker, W. (2000, c1991, c1994). *The complete word study Bible : King James Version.*